My
Favorite
Horses

WORKING
HORSES

Stephanie Turnbull

A⁺

Smart Apple Media

Published by Smart Apple Media,
an imprint of Black Rabbit Books
P.O. Box 3263, Mankato, Minnesota, 56002
www.blackrabbitbooks.com

Designed by Hel James
Edited by Mary-Jane Wilkins

Cataloging-in-Publication Data is available from the Library of Congress

ISBN 978-1-62588-180-9

Photo acknowledgements
t = top, b = bottom
title page stephen/Shutterstock.com; page 3 Shelli Jensen/Shutterstock;
4-5 Hemera/Thinkstock; 5 Vera Zinkova; 6 Zuzule/both Shutterstock;
8 Gregory Johnston; 9 Conny Sjostrom/both Shutterstock;
10-11 2xSamara.com, 10b murielbuzz/both Shutterstock;
12-13 PD Loyd/Shutterstock; 15t Zoran Karapancev/Shutterstock.com,
b Tatiana Morozova/Shutterstock; 16-17 justasc Shutterstock.com;
18-19 Jaroslaw Grudzinski/Shutterstock; 20 Moyakov; 21 Michael
G Smith/both Shutterstock; 22 Cheryl A. Meyer; 23t jo Crebbin,
b gorillaimages/all Shutterstock
Cover Vera Zinkova/Shutterstock

Printed in China

DAD0055
032014
9 8 7 6 5 4 3 2 1

Contents

Hard-Working Horses

Working horses can be big and strong or light and fast.

They are all calm, patient, and intelligent.

4

Horses can do all
kinds of useful jobs.

They may work in
the open countryside or
in the middle of busy cities.

Gentle Giants

The biggest, most powerful working horses are called draft or dray horses. They do hard, heavy work such as hauling loaded carts.

Percherons are alert, energetic French draft horses.

This is a Shire horse. It has long, thick leg hair called feathering, which helps keep it warm.

On the Farm

In the past, many horses worked on farms, plowing fields and pulling wagons. Some small farms still use horse power.

Teams of horses are attached to plows. As they plod steadily along, the plow blades loosen the soil, so it will be ready for planting seeds.

Loaded Down

Horses often carry food, tools, and other supplies along trails that are too steep or narrow for vehicles.

This horse is carrying firewood.

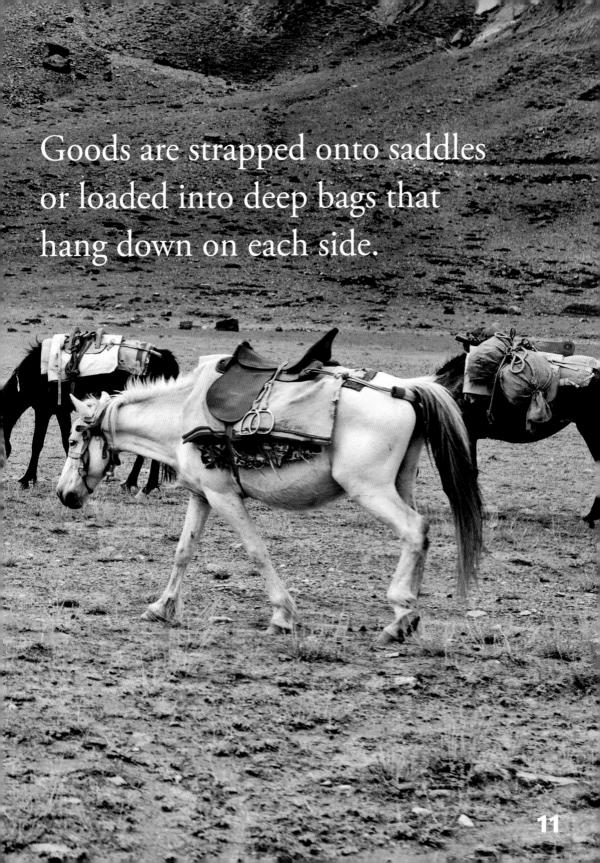

Goods are strapped onto saddles
or loaded into deep bags that
hang down on each side.

Ranch Horses

Some horses are ridden by cowboys on vast, open farms called ranches.

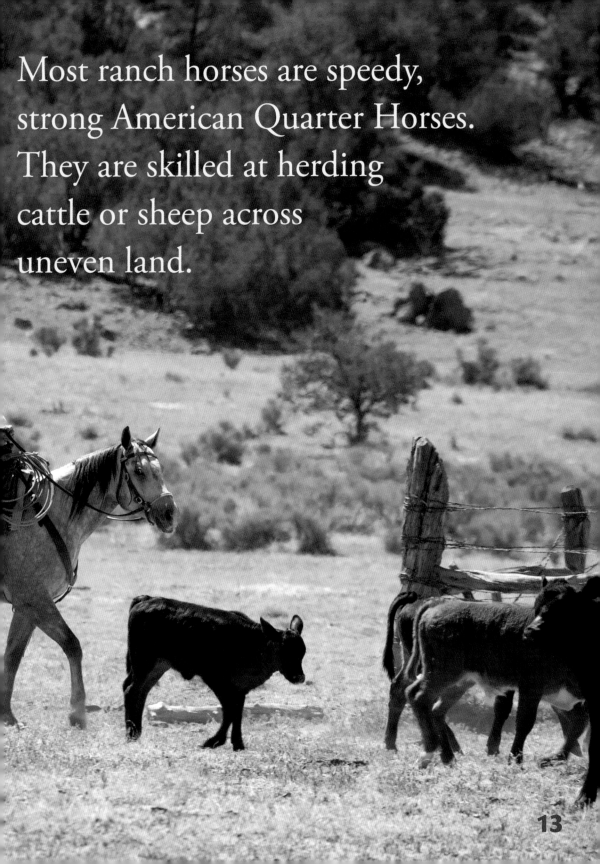

Most ranch horses are speedy, strong American Quarter Horses. They are skilled at herding cattle or sheep across uneven land.

Police Patrols

Police forces in many countries use horses to patrol streets and parks.

The Royal Canadian Mounted Police are famous for their elegant horses and uniforms. They often take part in special events.

Police in Moscow, Russia, also use horses.

Keeping Control

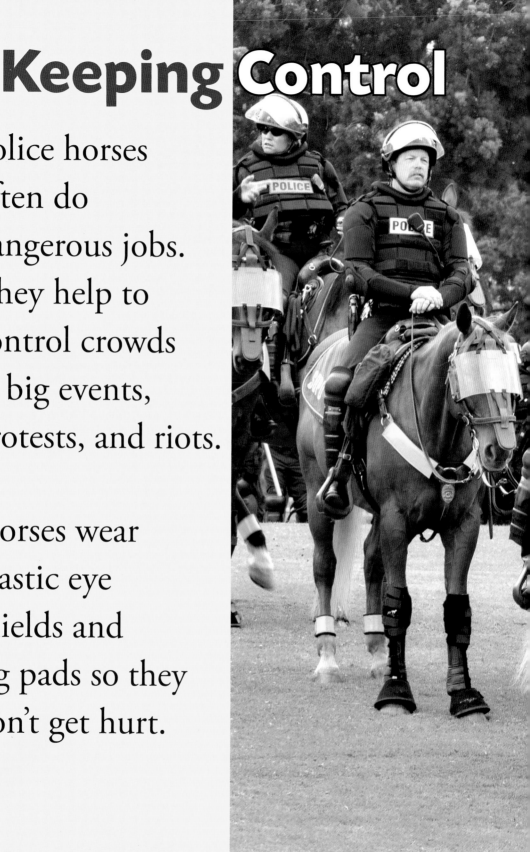

Police horses often do dangerous jobs. They help to control crowds at big events, protests, and riots.

Horses wear plastic eye shields and leg pads so they don't get hurt.

War Horses

In the past, soldiers galloped into battle on horseback.

Today, military horses are used in grand ceremonies. They know how to move gracefully and behave perfectly.

People Carriers

Many horses are trained
to carry people or
give them rides in
carriages or sleighs.

Some people prefer horses to motor vehicles. On Mackinac Island, in Michigan, cars are banned, so everyone uses horses to get around instead!

Helpful Horses

Some horses help rescuers search for lost or injured people in remote places.

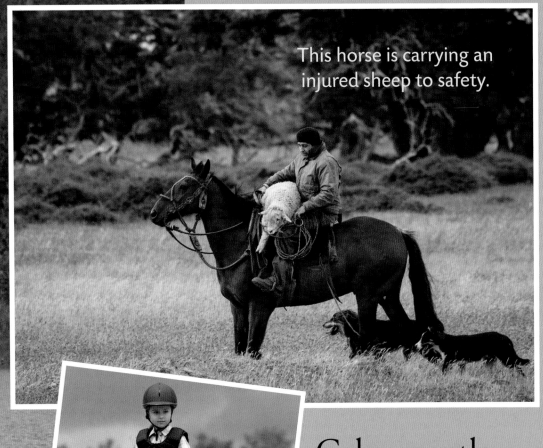

This horse is carrying an injured sheep to safety.

Calm, gentle horses help young children and people with disabilities learn to ride and have fun.

23

Useful Words

draft horse A big horse used to pull heavy loads.

patrol To keep watch over an area by walking through it.

plow Farm equipment with sharp blades that cut and turn soil.

ranch A huge area of land where farmers keep cattle or sheep.

Index